SCIENCE KIDS
Colors

RED

Pamela McDowell

LET'S READ AV² BY WEIGL™
ADDED VALUE • AUDIO VISUAL

Go to **www.av2books.com**, and enter this book's unique code.

BOOK CODE

X881581

AV² by Weigl brings you media enhanced books that support active learning.

AV² provides enriched content that supplements and complements this book. Weigl's AV² books strive to create inspired learning and engage young minds in a total learning experience.

Your AV² Media Enhanced books come alive with...

Audio
Listen to sections of the book read aloud.

Video
Watch informative video clips.

Embedded Weblinks
Gain additional information for research.

Try This!
Complete activities and hands-on experiments.

Key Words
Study vocabulary, and complete a matching word activity.

Quizzes
Test your knowledge.

Slide Show
View images and captions, and prepare a presentation.

... and much, much more!

Published by AV² by Weigl
350 5th Avenue, 59th Floor New York, NY 10118
Websites: www.av2books.com   www.weigl.com

Library of Congress Control Number: 2014934868

ISBN 978-1-4896-1262-5 (hardcover)
ISBN 978-1-4896-1263-2 (softcover)
ISBN 978-1-4896-1264-9 (single user eBook)
ISBN 978-1-4896-1265-6 (multi-user eBook)

Printed in the United States of America in North Mankato, Minnesota
1 2 3 4 5 6 7 8 9 0 18 17 16 15 14

042014
WEP150314

Project Coordinator: Aaron Carr
Designer: Mandy Christiansen

Weigl acknowledges Getty Images and iStock as the primary image suppliers for this title.

Science Kids
Colors

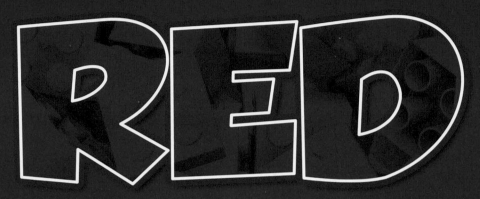

RED

CONTENTS

What is this color?
Do you know it? I do!

It is red that I see!
Can you see it too?

I see
a red pillow.

I see
a red bed.

What things in your house can you find that are red?

These berries
are sour.

These apples
are sweet.

Can you think of more red foods that you eat?

I see
a red car.

I see
a red doll.

Do you have a red wagon?
Do you have a red ball?

Look out in the garden.
Look up in the trees.

Do you see red flowers?
Do you see red leaves?

I see
a red butterfly.

I see
a red frog, too.

I see a red bird.
Is it singing for you?

I see
a red slide.

I see
a red swing.

At the playground
the tire is my favorite thing.

Is red found at school?
Have a good look.

I see
a red crayon.

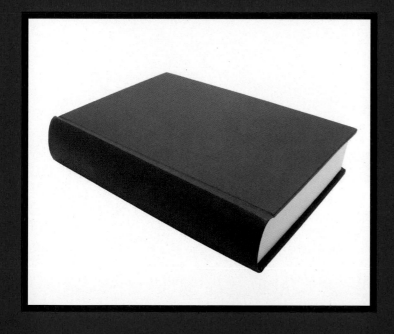

I see
a red book.

Red can
mean love.

Red can
mean hot.

Is there a red sign that you see a lot?

Find where these red things belong in this book.

Go back through the pages and have a close look!

KEY WORDS

Research has shown that as much as 65 percent of all written material published in English is made up of 300 words. These 300 words cannot be taught using pictures or learned by sounding them out. They must be recognized by sight. This book contains 49 common sight words to help young readers improve their reading fluency and comprehension. This book also teaches young readers several important content words, such as proper nouns. These words are paired with pictures to aid in learning and improve understanding.

Page	Sight Words First Appearance
4	do, I, is, it, know, this, what, you
5	can, see, that, too
6	a
7	are, find, house, in, things, your
8	these
9	eat, foods, more, of, think
10	car
11	have
12	look, out, the, trees, up
13	leaves
15	for
17	at, my
18	found, good, school
19	book
20	mean
21	there
22	where
23	and, back, close, go, pages, through

Page	Content Words First Appearance
4	color
5	red
6	bed, pillow
8	apples, berries
10	doll
11	ball, wagon
12	garden
13	flowers
14	butterfly, frog
15	bird
16	slide, swing
17	playground, tire
19	crayon
20	love
21	sign